GOOD FOR A LAUGH

A Guide to Writing
AMUSING, CLEVER,
and DOWNRIGHT
FUNNY Poems

ISBN 0-439-40963-2

12 11 10 9 8 7 6 5 4 3 2   3 4 5 6 7 8/0

Printed in the U.S.A.   40
First printing, May 2003

GOOD FOR A LAUGH

A Guide to Writing
AMUSING, CLEVER,
and DOWNRIGHT
FUNNY Poems

BY PAUL B. JANECZKO

SCHOLASTIC INC.

New York   Toronto   London   Auckland   Sydney
Mexico City   New Delhi   Hong Kong   Buenos Aires

With admiration and thanks
to these funny men who were good
for a laugh when I was a kid:
Steve Allen, Jack Benny,
Milton Berle, Sid Caesar,
Ernie Kovacs, Jean Shepherd
— P.B.J.

TABLE OF CONTENTS

LETTER FROM
THE AUTHOR

When I was your age, I didn't do very well in school. Part of the reason was that I didn't try very hard. Teachers constantly told my parents, "Paul just doesn't apply himself," as if I were some sort of paint. But one thing I did apply myself to was laughing. Whether it was trying to get a laugh from my classmates or my brothers, or laughing at the wacky and the weird in the world around me, I was good for a laugh. I was ready to say or do something funny. None of that has changed. I'm still ready to see, write, and say something funny.

When I started brainstorming ideas for this guide, I decided that I want to offer two things to young writers. First of all, I want to share with you the possibilities of humorous poetry. I'm pretty certain that you've chuckled and chortled over a Shel Silverstein poem or two. But because there is no one way to write humorous poetry, I want you to learn how to go beyond his poems to create your own funny poems and to feel the excitement of trying something new. Secondly, I want you to feel what it's like to have fun with language. I want you to delight in discovering the fun of puns and homonyms and exaggerations, and downright interesting words.

Some of the poems in this guide — as well as some of the poems that you'll write — will make people laugh out loud. On the other hand, some of them are more subtle* so people may react to these with a chuckle or a grin. The poems you write may be silly, clever, or amusing. Just remember that there are degrees of funniness, just as there are degrees on a thermometer.

After years of working with young writers as a high school English teacher and as a visiting poet at schools around the country, I felt it was time to try to write a guide that would give young writers some solid advice and suggestions (hopefully even some inspiration) on writing humorous poems. This is what you're holding in your hands right now. So, if you think there's a funny poet trapped inside your body that's dying to bust out, flip the page and start reading. As you write, I bet that you'll be good for a laugh!

Paul B. Janeczko
Hebron, Maine
Summer 2002

---

* **Subtle** is a nifty adjective that means not easily noticed.

GATHERING YOUR TOOLS

My father was the "tool king." He always seemed to have a new tool to take care of the calamities that happened around the house. And he always gave my brothers and me the same advice: Never use a tool to do something that it wasn't meant to do. This advice was usually dished out with a sigh after I used the handle of a screwdriver as a hammer or used a putty knife for freeing a slice of blackened bread caught in the maw of our temperamental toaster. My father also believed in buying quality tools. "Good tools," he was fond of saying to anyone who would listen, "will last you a lifetime."

Although I've tried to follow his advice on household tools, I realized that his advice applies to writing tools as well. When I write a poem or a book, I need good tools to help me do the job as well as I can. It's harder to write a good poem or a good book when you don't have the proper tools. No, that doesn't mean that you need to invest thousands of dollars in a state-of-the-art computer and printer. That's one of the good things about writing. You really don't need to spend a lot of money to get the tools you need. Oh, a computer is a great tool to have — and I'm glad to have a beauty — but other tools you need are much cheaper. And you can use the same tools if you are writing a funny poem or a thank-you letter to your Aunt Mildred in Muncie, Indiana, for the box of chocolate-covered grasshoppers she sent you for your birthday.

What tools will you need? First of all, I will tell you that I like writing tools of all sorts. On my desk are two cups filled with markers and pens of all colors and sizes. One of my desk drawers is lined with a rack of fountain pens, and I have another cup o' pens next to my computer. I want to make sure that when I'm ready to write — or highlight or draw or color — I have the right tools nearby. But to answer your question as simply as possible, I'd say you need a pen and a notebook. The rest is window dressing, but I will try to explain how these extras will fit into your writing. For now, the basics.

PEN

You'll need a pen. Obviously. Any pen that works for you will do. I like a fountain pen, but most people prefer a ballpoint pen or some sort of felt-tip marker. My daughter prefers to write her drafts with a pencil. It's a matter of personal choice, although most people don't give it too much thought. They just grab whatever is on the counter as they rush out the door. But pens are a lot like shoes (although they smell a lot better): You need to find a pen that's comfortable for you. If you're a lefty, that eliminates some markers because you will be dragging your writing fist through the wet ink. I say you want a comfortable pen because you don't want to be shaking cramps out of your writing hand every five minutes while you are working on your masterpiece. When it's time to buy a new pen, take the time to try out a couple different types. Remember: Pens are like shoes. Buy ones that feel good.

NOTEBOOK

Your writer's notebook will be your treasure chest into which you will write notes, observations, drafts, questions, lists, letters, jokes, favorite words, whatever. It's also the place where you can draw pictures and maps and diagrams and charts. Can you see why I say it's like a treasure chest? It will hold a lot of your secrets. But it also will be a place for you to try things out before you spring them on your audience. If you write in your notebook faithfully, you will find that it will become like a good friend to you. You will look forward to the time when you get to write in it. Like your pen, your notebook must be comfortable for you and serve your needs.

I suggest that you write in your notebook regularly. Does that mean everyday? For me it does. Every morning I get up an hour or so before my wife and daughter, and one of the things I do during that glorious quiet time is write in my journal. Most mornings I look forward to writing. I may write about what happened the day before. Sometimes I will write at length about one event. Other times I will write snatches of a conversation I heard at the corner store. I may lay out some of the things that I hope to accomplish that day.

The important thing is to write in the notebook. It doesn't have to be perfect. In fact, it won't be perfect. I don't know a single writer who gets it perfect the first time. Not one. That's one of the great things about writing in a notebook:

You don't have to worry about getting it "right." You just need to get it — whatever that "it" is on a given day — down on paper. Once you have it down on paper, you can fix it up. But before you can fix it, you need to write it down.

I have all sorts of notebooks. My morning notebook is one of those with 8" x 10" paper and a stiff marbled cover. That's "old faithful." I also keep a pocket-sized notebook in my car. Whenever I go for a walk, I make sure I take something to write with and something to write on, for observations or thoughts usually a file card folded in half. I keep a smaller notebook in the drawer of my bedside table. I have a medium-sized notebook that I carry with me when I travel. My travel notebook has saved me from boredom many times, especially one winter afternoon when I was stuck in the Cincinnati airport for five hours waiting for the next flight to Los Angeles. I jotted down ideas for books. I wrote a letter to my daughter. I wrote dialogue between two women who were sitting in the coffee shop across from my gate. I even tried to write some knock-knock jokes. *(Knock knock. Who's there? Barbie. Barbie who? Barbie Q.* Okay, I never said they were *good* knock-knock jokes!)

One of my friends uses a three-ring binder as her writer's notebook. It's too bulky for me, but it does allow her to rearrange the pages. Other people use small notebooks, although I think using a small notebook all the time tends to limit what you can write and draw. I like room to roam and expand.

MARKERS

I use highlighters in my notebook more than markers. I use them to call attention to something that I've written. For example, if I jot down a hilarious idea that I think is even more spectacular than my usual spectacular ideas, I run the ole neon yellow highlighter over it. It's like putting the idea on one of those Post-its. I also use highlighters to color code themes that run through my notebook. For example, if I'm writing down ideas for a new book of poems about my odd relatives, I might highlight that stuff with a green marker. Maybe I will highlight new book ideas in blue. The highlighters are great tools to help you organize and notice things in your notebook.

BOOKS

You should have three books nearby when you are writing.

Dictionary

A good, solid paperback edition will do fine. You don't need a fifteen-pound hardcover dictionary. I just bought a new paperback edition of the *American Heritage Dictionary*, and I keep it on my computer desk.

Thesaurus

Again, a good paperback edition will serve you well. It will list synonyms — words that mean the same thing — for just about any word you can think of. A good thesaurus will also include antonyms, which are words that mean the opposite.

Rhyming dictionary

Yes, there is such a thing, and it's exactly what it sounds like. You look up a word — *poodle,* for example — and it will list words that rhyme with *poodle.* (In case you're interested, those words are: *boodle, noodle, doodle, strudel, feudal, caboodle, flapdoodle, canoodle.)* Your school library probably has one in its reference collection. But you can also buy a good one like *The Scholastic Rhyming Dictionary*, which contains a whopping 15,000 words!

Your computer is probably loaded with a dictionary and a thesaurus, but I still think you should have a paperback copy of each on your desk. There are two reasons for that. First, chances are the computer versions do not contain as many entries as the book versions. Second, it's fun to page through a rhyming dictionary and take note of the neat words you will find along the way. Don't take the easy way out and rely on the computer versions. Buy your own books for your desk. Or ask your Aunt Mildred in Muncie, Indiana, for a paperback dictionary for your next birthday (unless you'd rather have those chocolate-covered grasshoppers again).

You need to read poetry if you are going to write it. Period. Trust me on this one. I can't name one writer who is not a reader. You practice writing poems by actually writing them. You also practice, in a sense, by reading poems. So, get yourself to the library and see what books of poetry you can discover. You can also ask your teacher or your librarian for suggestions. If you have a couple of favorite poets, track down their books on the shelves. Read, read, read. By carefully reading what other poets have written, we can learn the *how* of their poems. You can even learn from the poems that you don't like. When you write, you will imitate the best that you have read. Imitation is okay when you are starting to do anything. Over time and with — here comes the p-word — practice, you will develop your own writing voice and style. Don't be afraid to learn from other poets, especially the ones you admire.

THE WRITING PROCESS

Do you have to follow the writing process to write funny poems? I think so. If you don't, I suspect you'll find yourself rushing through your writing. And I've learned that hurrying is one of the surest ways to wreck something, whether you're building a deck, learning a magic trick, or writing a limerick.

Will following the writing process guarantee that you'll write terrific poems? Of course not. No more than knowing how to throw a curve ball will guarantee that you'll pitch a no-hitter every time. It takes patience and practice to do most things well. Writing is one of them. And patience in writing means that you take the time to follow the writing process.

Understand that when I say that it's important to follow the writing process, I'm not saying that it'll be the same for every writer. Nor am I saying that you'll spend the same amount of time on each step in the process whenever you write. I am saying, however, that you should follow the *process,* follow the writing steps each time you write. Good writing — whether it's a hilarious poem or a letter of apology — takes time. Give yourself time to consider each step along the way.

Chances are your teachers have talked about the writing process in class. Although they may have used slightly different words for each step, the writing process generally involves five stages: brainstorm, draft, revise, proofread, and publish.

BRAINSTORM

Between you and me, this is the part of the writing process that I enjoy the most — when the words and ideas are flying around the room and landing in my notebook. When you brainstorm, try not to stop yourself from putting an idea down in your notebook because you think it's "not good" or "stupid." When you brainstorm, there are no bad ideas. The whole point is to let your imagination run loose.

DRAFT

This is when you start writing down ideas in a way that makes sense for you. You want your first draft to be as good as you can get it, but you don't want to stop the writing flow to look up the spelling of words or check with your mother to see if Aunt Mildred was born in Havana or Hoboken. You'll check all of that stuff later when you revise.

REVISE

Here's where the real work of writing happens. Your poem will only be as good as you are willing to revise it. This is a good time to read your poem to your writing partner, which I will talk about later on. Let your partner listen to it and suggest ways in which it can be improved. It's also a good idea to put your poem away for a couple of weeks and not look at it. After it's had a chance to sit alone in a dark file drawer, take it out and read it again. Is it as good as you thought it was? Can you find things that need to be changed?

PROOFREAD

When you have made all the revisions that you are going to make to your poem, it's time to go over it another time to check for spelling, capitalization, punctuation, sentence structure, and subject-verb agreement. By this time, you have probably put a lot of work into your poem, so don't spoil it by not proofreading it carefully.

PUBLISH

Once you have worked through the writing process on your poem, you'll probably be very proud of your work. As you should be. So, why not share your poem with others? There are a number of ways to do that, and I will suggest some throughout this book.

Don't forget what I said before: The writing process is not exactly the same for everyone. Nor will it be exactly the same for you every time you write a poem. However, the steps are important because they give you the best opportunity to write a good poem. So, don't cheat yourself or your reader by speeding through the steps. Just chill.

WHAT YOU'LL FIND
IN THIS BOOK

All of the poems that I've included as models in this book are written in a particular form, whether it's the short three-line senryu or the couplets of "Ten Little Aliens." This is not meant to give the impression that funny poems need to follow a poetic form. Although many funny poems follow a pattern (hello, Jack Prelutsky and Shel Silverstein!), I decided to base this guide on poems that follow poetic forms because I think to have to write within the limits of a poetic form often helps young writers. Why? Because it limits what you can do. It also helps you focus your thinking and your writing. Having said that, I hereby give you complete permission to expand and tinker with these forms . . . *after* you have tried to write the forms as they are presented. After using these poetic forms with hundreds of students in writing workshops across the country, I can guarantee that you will have a lot of laughs writing these poems. Trust me.

For each poetic form, I include a model poem so that you can read an example of the form. In addition, you'll find the following sections:

 What Makes It Work: An explanation of the specific qualities of each type of humorous poem

 Brainstorm: A suggestion to jump-start your imagination

 Writing Tips: Tidbits to help you write your poem

 Practice: A chance to try out some aspect of the poem

 For Your Notebook: Suggestions on how to make your writer's notebook a valuable asset as you grow as a writer

 Wordplay: Clever and entertaining word games that will allow you to expand your writing vocabulary

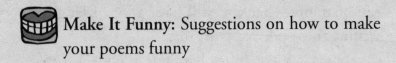

Make It Funny: Suggestions on how to make your poems funny

As you can see, there is plenty of material to help you write funny poems. Take the time to enjoy each section.

A FEW WORDS ABOUT PUBLISHING

Chances are that when you hear the word publishing, you think of a book. Or maybe a magazine. But there are a number of ways to publish your humorous poems.

- The most obvious way to publish your poems is to print them out and distribute them to friends and family.

- Short poems — like senryus and opposites — are perfectly suited to put on a small card to give to someone or to drop in the mail. (A funny poem can do wonders to lift someone's spirits.)

- With a little paper folding and cutting, you can put a number of your poems into a small booklet.

- You can turn longer poems — like "I Made a Mistake," "Ten Little Aliens," and "If I Could

Put a Curse on You" — into posters. You might even consider illustrating your poster.

All of these publishing ideas have one thing in common: They involve a printed poem. But don't feel limited to printing your poem when you think of publishing it. You can record your poems on a cassette and give it to someone. (Wouldn't your Aunt Mildred just love to pinch your cheek in appreciation if you sent her a recording of you reading some of your funny poems!) You could also recite your poems to a live audience. And many of the poems can be easily recited with a friend in a lively, back-and-forth fashion. Just make sure someone videotapes your performance.

Don't be limited by my suggestions. Use your imagination to come up with unique and zany ways to share your funny poems with the world. Hey, we all know that the world could use a good laugh.

FINALLY, SOMETHING FOR FREE

FREE ADVICE #1

Save your poems. Even the ones that are half-baked. Even the ones that you think aren't very good. You never know when you may get back to one of them and put the finishing touches on it. This will be more and more likely to happen as you become a better poet.

Of course, the poems you really want to save are the finished ones. The ones you are nuts about. Saving them in a computer file goes without saying. But I think it's also important to print your finished poems, punch three holes in them, and stick them in a binder. You will be surprised how your sense of satisfaction and pride will grow — not to mention your confidence as a poet — as you see that binder thicken with your poems.

FREE ADVICE #2

Although it may be hard for you to set up a specific time to practice your writing, it's a good thing if you can. Even though I write in short bursts in hotel rooms, on airplanes, and in the car while I'm waiting for my daughter to get out of soccer practice, I like to know when I sit down to write that I will have a nice stretch of time to do my work. I am a strong believer in the "Groove Factor," which states that, more often than not, when you get into a writing groove, good things will happen. So, try to give yourself enough time for the Groove Factor to kick in.

FREE ADVICE #3

Try to work with a writing partner. Some of the funniest TV shows and movies are the work of writing teams because it does help to bounce funny ideas — and the occasional wad of crumpled paper — off a writing partner. Even if that person tells you on occasion that your poem isn't funny, that may, in fact, be helpful. What will happen is that your partner may say, "Okay, but how about this?" and offer a good suggestion. To which you can say, "That might work if I do this," and tweak her idea a bit. Which is not to say that you *have* to write with a partner. Or that you *have* to write with a partner all the time. It's only to say that sometimes it helps to write funny stuff if you work with a partner. It's up to you, but here are some suggestions:

- Since many of the poems in this book are written in couplets — like "Ten Little Aliens" and "If I Could Put a Curse on You" — you might want to write the first line and have your partner write the second line of the couplet.

- A couple of the poems, like "I Made a Mistake" and "When I Grow Up," are perfectly suited to a kind of can-you-top-this game with a partner. You know, where you write a couplet or stanza and challenge your partner to write a funnier one.

- And, of course, it's a good idea to read your poems to a writing partner and see if she can notice something that needs work. Or, she just might pat you on the back and cry, "Nice job!"

FREE ADVICE #4

This book is not set up in any sort of sequential manner. In other words, one poem does not build on what you did with another. Along the way, I have highlighted some words in **boldface** and tried to explain them. So feel free to pick and choose your way through this book. When you find a type of poem that works for you, give it some time and practice it before you move on. Or, you can work your way through the book trying each poem in succession, and then go back and spend more time on the ones that you especially liked.

FREE ADVICE #5

Most of the types of poems that I include in this book follow a pretty definite form. However, don't be afraid to tinker with the forms or tweak them a bit as an experiment. First, try the poetic form as first presented. Then, see if you need to change it a bit to fit your imagination. In other words, don't be a slave to poetic forms.

1

I MADE A MISTAKE

Any coach who's worth her salt will always have her athletes warm up before they start any rigorous practice. Warming up loosens your muscles, reducing the likelihood of an injury. Well, I've found that the same thing is true with writing. No, I'm not going to ask you to drop and give me twenty-five push-ups. But it's usually a good idea to warm up with words, as a way of getting language flowing, of getting your creativity cranking. With that in mind, let me offer a simple rhyme that you can use to get your imagination and rhyming mechanism warmed up.

Model Poem

I MADE A MISTAKE

(A Jump-rope Rhyme)

I went to the closet to pick out a tie,
I made a mistake . . . and discovered a spy.

I went to the park to enjoy the slide,
I made a mistake . . . and rode out on the tide.

I went outside to visit Ginny,
I made a mistake . . . and landed in New Guinea.

I went to the garden to pick a bloom,
I made a mistake . . . and fell in a tomb.

I went to my friend's to do something crude,
I made a mistake . . . and he got sued.

I went to the stage to sing the blues,
I made a mistake . . . and lost my shoes.

I went to the store to buy some cheese,
I made a mistake . . . and forgot to say please.

I went to the laundry to wash my shirt,
I made a mistake . . . and started to flirt.

I went to the sea to go for a sail,
I made a mistake . . . and got caught in a gale.

I went to the zoo to see the fox,
I made a mistake . . . and he stole my socks.

I went to the mountain to ski down the slope,
I made a mistake . . . and slipped on the soap.

I went to school to learn some math,
I made a mistake . . . and took a bath.

I went next door to marry Raquel,
I made a mistake . . . and said farewell.

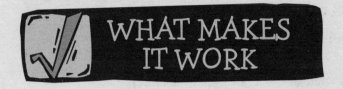

WHAT MAKES
IT WORK

Like most rhyming poems — you'll see this over and over in the model poems in this guide — "I Made a Mistake" follows a pattern. Do you notice an aspect of the poem that follows a pattern?

Before you answer that question, ask yourself this one: *Have I read the poem out loud?* If your answer is no, don't do another thing until you read "I Made a Mistake" out loud. You don't have to read it to anybody — although I have found that cats and certain species of parrots make great listeners — but it's nice to read it to somebody. Try reading it to a friend.

Why should you read out loud? Good question. My answer: Poetry is meant to be read aloud if you want to hear all that it has to offer. Oh, you can read a poem and understand it, but you won't hear all the music of the poem unless you read it out loud. The music of poetry comes from rhythm, rhyme, word choice, and word order. And you can best hear those things when you hear the words with your ears, rather than just in your head. Read all the model poems in this book aloud before you try to write your own. When you're a rich and famous poet, you'll thank me. Actually, you'll thank me long before that. You'll thank me every time you read a poem aloud and hear its music.

What did you notice about the patterns in this poem? More than likely, you noticed:

- The poem is made up of **couplets.** (A couplet is a pair of lines that have **end rhyme,** which means the words at the end of the lines rhyme, or, in other words, they sound alike. For example, *bear* and *hair, friend* and *end.* Easy, right?)
- The first line of each couplet begins with the phrase, *I went.*
- The second line of each couplet begins with the phrase, *I made a mistake . . . and.*
- Each couplet follows the same rhythm (which you will hear and feel if you read the poem out loud). In other words, each couple sounds alike.

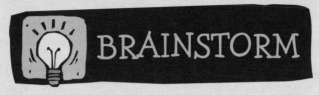

BRAINSTORM

There are three parts to the story that you tell in each couplet. Brainstorm ideas for the first two parts by writing two columns in your notebook and labeling them as follows:

Where did you go?   **Why did you go there?**

The information you write in these columns will wind up in the first line of your poem. For example, *I went next door to marry Raquel.* Once you have the first parts written in the columns, you are ready to write a rhyming line that will complete the couplet. Try to write enough for 6 to 8 couplets.

WRITING TIPS

TIP #1

Think of each couplet as a very teeny tiny short story. In the first line you went someplace (e.g., *I went to the closet*, *I went to the park)* to do something (e.g., *to pick out a tie, to enjoy the slide).* In the second line, you made a mistake and did something else (e.g., *discovered a spy, rode out on the tide*).

TIP #2

You don't need to use the same verb in both lines of the poem. In fact, if you change the verb in the second line, you will often get a funnier couplet. For example, in the second couplet of the model poem, the verb in the first line is *enjoy*, while the verb in the second line is *rode out*. The usage of different verbs is one reason why that couplet is humorous. By choosing a different verb, you'll surprise the reader, and surprise is often an element of "funny."

PRACTICE

Here are some first lines of couplets for "I Made a Mistake." After thinking about my first line, write a second line for each couplet. Make sure that each line makes sense.

　1.　I went to the store to buy some bread,
　　　I made a mistake . . . and _____.

2. I went outside to look at the stars,
   I made a mistake . . . and _____.
3. I went to the ocean to find a shell,
   I made a mistake . . . and _____.
4. I went to my school to learn to read,
   I made a mistake . . . and _____.
5. I went to the mall to buy some shoes,
   I made a mistake . . . and _____.

Now that you've had a chance to brainstorm some opening lines and to practice writing some rhyming lines, it's time for you to try writing complete couplets. You can take the opening lines that you wrote for the brainstorming exercise and write second lines.

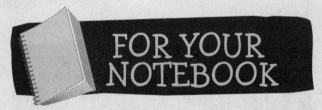

FOR YOUR NOTEBOOK

Why not set aside a page or two of your notebook for interesting rhymes? I wouldn't bother collecting your simple garden-variety rhyming words, like *cat* and *bat,* or *flow* and *know.* I'd go for the more intriguing rhymes, like *smirk* and *jerk,* or *anxiety* and *notoriety.* Keep your ears alert to new rhymes. Or, if you discover a word that you like — *cemetery,* let's say — but can't find a rhyme for, ask a friend for help. A rhyming dictionary also comes in handy in times like this!

WORDPLAY

The granddaddy of all rhyming word games might be "Hink Pink," or its cousin, "Hinky Pinky." The basic rules are simple: one player thinks of a phrase that is made of two single-syllable rhyming words, like *hot tot.* That player says, "I am thinking of a Hink Pink," then briefly describes the Hink Pink: "It's a very warm baby." The other player tries to come up with the answer. The secret is to work backward. In other words, think of pairs of rhyming words, then look for a way you can express their connection as a "Hink Pink."

Here are a couple of other examples:

A: I'm thinking of a Hink Pink.
  It's an angry employer.
B: Cross boss.
A: I'm thinking of a Hink Pink.
  It's an obese feline.

B: Fat cat.

"Hinky Pinky" follows the same rules, but the answers are phrases with two-syllable rhymes. A "Hinky Pinky" would go like this:

A: I'm thinking of a Hinky Pinky.

   It's a convenient confection.

B: Handy candy.

A: I'm thinking of a Hinky Pinky.

   It's a very slim girl named Virginia.

B: Skinny Ginny

So, grab a friend or your writing partner and starting thinking up some rhyming words for this game. Have fun!

MAKE IT FUNNY

I will remind you from time to time through this guide that a good poet is a good observer. So, if you want to find funny things to write about — or if you want to find things that you can write about and make funny — take a look around you. Grab a small notebook and observe. Take notes. Go to the school cafeteria and watch the way people act. See something that could make a funny poem? I bet you do! Open your ears when you are on the school bus. Do you hear any funny conversations? Write them down. Observe at the grocery store. Observe your older brother with his friends. Observe your little sister with her friends. Notice things that happen around the dinner table, on the bench during a soccer game, in the library, the classroom, and at the mall. Observe and take notes. As you write your way through the activities in this book, you will return to your observations over and over again for material for your poems.

WHEN I GROW UP

A lot of the poets who I find funny happen to live "across the pond" in England. One of the funnier ones is Colin McNaughton. He's published about sixty books, many of which he has written *and* comically illustrated. One of the poems, from *Who's Been Sleeping in My Porridge?: A Book of Wacky Poems and Pictures,* that I like very much is "When I Grow Up." I think my version of this poem below makes another good "warm-up" poem.

Model Poem

WHEN I GROW UP
(after Colin McNaughton)

When I grow up
I would like to be
chased about for
piracy.

When I grow up
I would like to be
squeaky clean and
sanitary.

When I grow up
I would like to be
the last one to
the cemetery.

When I grow up
I would like to be
an usher in
the balcony.

When I grow up
I would like to be

a banger of
a timpani.*

When I grow up
I would like to be
known for my brave
chivalry.

When I grow up
I would like to be
captured in a
tapestry.

* A **timpani** is a set of kettledrums usually found in a symphony orchestra.

WHAT MAKES IT WORK

As you can tell, this is another rhyming poem that follows a pattern. The pattern is not as rigid as the pattern in "I Made a Mistake." When you read the poem out loud — you haven't forgotten that you're supposed to do that, have you? — you can hear a pattern that includes these things:

- Each **stanza** contains four lines. (A stanza is a group of lines in a poem that is separated from other groups by a space. It's like a paragraph in prose writing.)

- The first two lines of each stanza are always the same: *When I grow up/I would like to be.*

- In each stanza the second and the fourth lines rhyme.

- The second line always ends with *be,* which means that the fourth line of the stanza must end with a word that ends with the *ee* sound.

- Every stanza has the same rhythm.

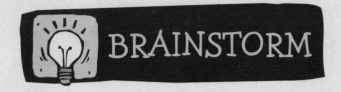

BRAINSTORM

Come up with a list of things you would like to do in life. You could write down occupations, but you could also write down some wild things, like *fly in space*. These ideas don't need to be written to fit into the poem. But you could do so. For example, if I wanted to take my idea — *fly in space* — and rewrite it so it would fit into the poem by rhyming with *be,* I might write *fly around in the galaxy.* Then, when I draft my poem, I might come up with this stanza:

When I grow up
I would like to be
a traveler in
the galaxy.

WRITING TIPS

Since "When I Grow Up" could be a poem about occupations, you might want to see what

38

occupations or occupation-related words you can think of that have the long *e* sound at the end of them. *Dictionary, cemetery,* and *culinary* are a few that come to mind. When you come up with such words, write them down on a page in your notebook. It's a good idea to label that page so you know why you wrote those words. I like to label my notes with the name of the poem the notes go with. So, I'd probably label this page WHEN I GROW UP. Whenever you think of something that might fit into a poem, you could add it to the list.

PRACTICE

Since you'll need to rhyme with the long *e* sound that's in the word *be,* you might want to practice coming up with words and phrases that rhyme with that sound. You could set up a page in your notebook by writing across the top: WHEN I GROW UP, I'D LIKE TO BE . . . Below it you can list words and phrases that rhyme with it, like

- a wonderful star on TV
- someone blessed with ESP
- a racer in a grand prix

- mellow and fancy-free
- a dispenser of sweet iced tea

Once you get the hang of the rhythm and rhyme of these lines, you will have no trouble writing a dozen or so good ones. Then you can rewrite them on a sheet of paper, following the pattern of the model poem.

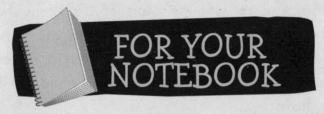

FOR YOUR NOTEBOOK

One of the best things you can do when you are writing a funny poem is to "stand the model on its head." For example, you might want to write a "When I Grow Up" poem about things you'd never want to do. When I was younger and got discouraged about my job, I would make a list of things I would never want to do. The first thing on my list was *foot doctor.* I couldn't imagine looking at people's feet all day. Yuck! By the time I was finished making my list, I usually felt better. So, you might want to write a poem that follows the pattern of "When I Grow Up," but the second line of each stanza would be, "I would hate to be."

WORDPLAY

"The Undertaker's Rat" may have started on a school playground a long time ago. Some people call it "The Minister's Cat." In this game, you describe a rat — its name and a descriptive word must begin with the same letter. I might begin by saying (or writing), *The undertaker owns an adorable rat whose name is Annette.* (Notice that *adorable* and *Annette* begin with *a*.) Your partner would then say something like, *The undertaker owns a belligerent rat whose name is Benjamin.* This goes on with both of you trying to continue the game by coming up with interesting adjectives and names as you go through the alphabet.

If you really want a challenge, you can make the game more interesting by including two adjectives in each line. You might come up with something like this:

The undertaker owns . . .

an adorable and affable rat whose name is Arnold.

a beneficial and boisterous rat whose name is Bertha.

a careless and cantankerous rat whose name is Calvin.

If you are interested in making the game even more challenging, you can include two adjectives that are somewhat contradictory. For example:

The undertaker owns . . .

an adorable but apathetic rat whose name is Alvin.

a boastful but beautiful rat whose name is Beatrice.

a cranky but cuddly rat whose name is Carl.

MAKE IT FUNNY

What makes you laugh? You've probably never stopped to think about that before. Well, now's the time. What people on TV and in the movies make you laugh? Can you think of funny books that you've read? What parts did you find funny? Why? Are there situations that you find funny? What about your best friends? Do they find the same things funny as you do? Have you ever purposely made kids in your class laugh? What did you do? What did you say?

Take a few minutes to write the answers to

some of these questions in your notebook. Don't look at this exercise as some sort of test with a "right" or a "wrong" answer. Rather, it's meant to get you thinking a little bit about what sorts of things make you and your friends laugh, or at least snicker. You might discover something that you can use when you write the poems in this book.

I'D RATHER BE

This poem came about from a word game that I played with my daughter one summer when we were on vacation. We would sit on the porch as the sun was going down and enjoy the competitive back-and-forth of this fun game. Later I realized that it could be made into an amusing rhyming poem. Since then, it's a poem that I always take with me when I visit schools and work with kids.

Model Poem

I'D RATHER BE

I'd rather be hands than feet.
I'd rather be honest than cheat.
I'd rather be cold than heat.
I'd rather be Paul than Pete.
I'd rather be a bed than a seat.
I'd rather be a blanket than a sheet.
I'd rather be corn than wheat.
I'd rather be a woof than a tweet.
I'd rather be a trick than a treat.
I'd rather be sunshine than sleet.
I'd rather be wood than concrete.
I'd rather be huge than petite.
I'd rather be sad than upbeat.
I'd rather be new than repeat.
I'd rather be tart than sweet.
I'd rather be a road than a street.
I'd rather be fun than compete.
I'd rather be veggies than meat.
I'd rather be a carrot than a beet.

WHAT MAKES IT WORK

This rhyming poem follows a pattern much the way the first two poems do. But do you notice how "I'd Rather Be" is different from the others? Do you notice the following things?

- The sound of the end words — *eet* — is the same in each line, so each line has end rhyme.
- Each line begins with the same phrase: *I'd rather be.*
- Each line has a similar rhythm.

These are the most obvious aspects of the pattern of this poem. But did you notice that most lines are about opposites? If not exact opposites, then things that are at least contradictory. For example, here are some **opposites:** *tart/sweet, huge/petite, cold/heat.* Here are a few words from the poem that are **contradictory:** *wood/concrete, road/street, blanket/sheet.* So, the important thing to remember is that "I'd Rather Be" is a poem about *differences.*

BRAINSTORM

One way to begin writing your poem is to brainstorm a list of opposites or a list of things that are somewhat different. Draw a line down the center of a page in your notebook. Write a word in the left-hand column, then write its opposite in the other column. You can start with a list of things that have obvious differences. For example:

hot   cold, ice
cold   heat, the sun, fire
window   door
curtain   drapes, shade
light   heavy, dark

Once you've made your list, you can begin to see which ones can be combined in a line of poetry that follows the pattern and rhythm of the model poem. But make sure you go beyond the obvious. If you pay attention, you will find things on your list that you didn't intend to use in a poem, but there they are! For example, from my short sample list above I might wind up saying things like:

I'd rather be fire than ice.
I'd rather be a drape than a shade.

I'd rather be an ounce than a pound.
I'd rather be a shade than a lamp.
I'd rather be open than shut.

The point is that you need to look at different meanings for any words that you brainstorm. For example, *shade* can be that thing that goes on a lamp, or a thing that keeps the sun out of your window, or what you can sit in under a huge tree. This poem gives you a chance to really examine the different meanings words have.

WRITING TIPS

TIP #1

Since this poem is based on the same end rhyme sound, it might help if you could come up with some sounds for which there are a lot of words. Let me give you some sounds to show you what I mean:

sound	words
-un	won, stun, one, son
-at	cat, hat, rat, diplomat
-ew	IQ, stew, debut, ah-choo

-ee flee, agree, carefree, M.D.

-ake bake, ache, opaque, cupcake

I especially like rhyming words that aren't spelled the same, like *bake/ache, you/debut, won/shun.* I love it when poets surprise me this way.

TIP #2

A variation of this poem is to write it in couplets, like "I Made a Mistake," rather than having every line end with the identical sound. A couplet version of the poem might begin this way:

I'd rather be moon than sun.
I'd rather be many than none.

I'd rather be soda than punch.
I'd rather be a fact than a hunch.

Get it? Every two lines will have end rhyme, rather than every line ending with the same sound.

Here are a few couplets with some words missing. See if you can find words that would make them work:

1. I'd rather be a veggie than _____.
   I'd rather be _____ than feet.
2. I'd rather be a chef than a _____.
   I'd rather be Pan than _____.
3. I'd rather be free than a _____.
   I'd rather be _____ than brave.
4. I'd rather be clear than _____.
   I'd rather be a _____ than a log.
5. I'd rather be a _____ than a belt.
   I'd rather be solid than _____.

After you've worked on these practice couplets, try to write your own poem.

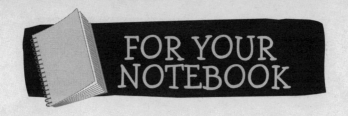

Working on this poem will give you the opportunity to look up words in the thesaurus. Then you can think of opposites to use in your lines. For example, here are a few words I found in my thesaurus when I looked up the word *strong:* powerful, hardy, brawny, sturdy, muscular. Now, I can write something like:

I'd rather be weak than brawny.
I'd rather be buff than scrawny.

Remember that the dictionary and the thesaurus are parts of your writer's toolbox, so don't be afraid to use them. They include lots of words that you know but may not think to use at a particular moment. Looking up words in these reference books is a good way to learn more about your language. When you are writing funny poems, don't be afraid to try something new. Take risks. You might amaze yourself with what you come up with.

WORDPLAY

There are times when I work with kids in writing workshops and I declare a ban on such verbs as *went, got,* or *said.* What's wrong with these verbs? Absolutely nothing, except that they often give writers an easy way out. For instance, instead of trying to find a more vivid verb — like *ambled, crawled, sauntered,* or even *ran, walked, strolled* — they settle for *went.* "Alphabetical Verbs" is a word game that helps you learn more vivid verbs.

You can play this game by yourself or with a partner. You can even play it with a group of your friends. Look at this sample:

A ambled to the store for a newspaper.

B broke her fingernail while fixing a flat tire.

C chitchatted with her mother on the phone.

D dug for buried treasure on the beach.

Get it? You simply write sentences that have a capital letter doing something. That doing — the verb — must begin with the same letter that starts the sentence. In my sample, A *ambled,* B *broke,* C *chitchatted,* and D *dug.* And so on through the alphabet.

You can make this game more challenging if you use at least one other word in the chain that begins with the same letter as the subject of the sentence. For example:

A ambled to the store for an anvil.

B broke her fingernail while blowing up a
　flat tire.

C chitchatted with her mother on the
　phone with a calling card.

D dug for buried treasure on the deserted
　beach.

My favorite variation of this game is to have all the sentences tell a story:

A arrived with a packed car.

B began to unpack.

C carried the tent to the perfect spot.

D dawdled making a campfire.

I hope you can see how much fun this game is! And you'll learn some vivid verbs in the process, which will only help your writing.

MAKE IT FUNNY

When I was a kid, there was one game, aside from baseball, that my friends and I loved to play. It was a "can-you-top-this?" game. In other words, it was an exercise in exaggeration, which has long been a way to get a laugh. Someone would start things rolling by saying something like, "My sister is so short." Someone else, with a smile on his lips, would ask, "How short is she?" And then we were treated to a whopper that often had us doubled over in laughter. It was all good-natured ribbing and, even though we never knew it, that sort of language play gave us a chance to practice our exaggeration.

Here are a couple of examples to give you an idea of how exaggeration can be funny:

My sister is so short that . . .

> she can play handball on the curb.
> she can hang glide on a potato chip.
> she can take a bath in a thimble.
> she can surf on a popsicle stick.
> she has to reach up to tie her shoes.

My uncle is so old that . . .

    he drove a chariot to the prom.

    his memory is in black and white.

    he owes a caveman a quarter.

    his candles cost more than his birthday cake.

    his social security number is 1.

When you're ready to have some laughs, try exaggerating!

I'D LIKE TO

If you're like me, you spend a fair amount of time (okay, on some days *a lot* of time) daydreaming. I sometimes imagine things that I'd like to do. Play baseball in the major leagues. Write a book that sells a zillion copies. Take trips to exotic places. One day I interrupted my daydreaming and started writing down some of my fantasies. It was an interesting list. Then, I fooled around with it some more and started adding rhyme and rhythm, and made a poem. Before long I'd written "I'd Like to . . ."

Model Poem

I'D LIKE TO

Eat a watermelon whole
Take an ostrich for a stroll

Jump around on cherry Jell-O
Call the Prez to say hello

Put the grades on my report card
Feast on pasta by the yard

Send my parents off to bed
Lock my sister in the shed

Get someone to clean my room
Have a classy nom de plume*

Pitch a shutout in the Bigs
Write some poems that you can dig

*A **nom de plume** is French for "pen name."

WHAT MAKES IT WORK

This poem is written in couplets. But there is more to it than that. "I'd Like to" is a far-fetched list, but that's the point. It should be something of a fantasy list. Things you'd love to do. Notice that some of the things in the poem are more fanciful than others; for example, "Eat a watermelon whole/Take an ostrich for a stroll." Others may be more closely related to your life, as in "Send my parents off to bed/Lock my sister in the shed."

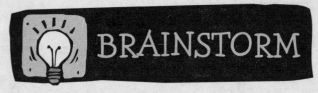

BRAINSTORM

"I'd Like to" gives you a chance to let your imagination run wild and brainstorm some of the things that you'd love to do. Probably things you'll never be able to do in your life. They can be things that deal with your life at home, like *Never have to do my chores* or *Run a mile in nothing flat*. Or, they can be related to school, such as *Read a book in 20 seconds* or *Sit behind the cutest girl*. Or, your ideas can be really out there: *Drive a rocket to the moon* or *Win an Oscar for my film*. It doesn't matter if your ideas are crazy. You're brainstorming. Anything goes! So, start making a list of your fantasies. Keep your fantasies short, so if you find you have something that might work in your poem you won't have to do too much tinkering.

WRITING TIPS

Although the brainstorming part of this poem is lots of fun, don't forget that you need to write your final poem in couplets. However, don't let that stop you from writing down an idea when you hear that little voice in the back of your head tell you, "Are you nuts?! You'll never come up with a word that rhymes with *girl*." Don't listen to that voice. Just write down every good line that comes to mind. After you've written about a dozen lines, you can start worrying about writing lines that will rhyme with the ones you've already written. (By the way, won't that little voice be surprised when you write *Take a dive and find a pearl* to go with *Sit behind the cutest girl*?)

PRACTICE

How about a little practice? Write rhyming lines to go with these "I'd Like to" lines:

1. Learn to play exquisite cello.
2. Get good news about my weight.
3. Parachute into a pool.
4. Find a loaded diamond mine.
5. Eat my lunch in the Eiffel Tower.

Can you write some outrageous lines that will rhyme with these lines? Give it a try. When you have written some good rhyming lines in your notebook, try to write your own "I'd Like to" poem.

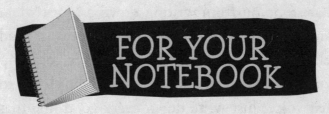

FOR YOUR NOTEBOOK

Pay attention to your fantasies. Write them down in your notebook. When you find yourself saying, "I wish I could . . ." or "Wouldn't it be great if I could . . . ," that's the time to pay attention because it sounds like a fantasy is about to appear on your radar screen. When it does, nab it and save it in your notebook. You can also brain-storm a list of things you would write to complete ideas like these: *If I led a perfect life . . .* or *If only I could . . .* In fact, you might want to save a page or two in your notebook for such fantasies.

WORDPLAY

A word game that can help your rhyming is "Rhyming Conversation." Like many of the other word games included in this book, this one is pretty simple: you carry on a conversation by replying with a rhyme to what has been asked by the previous person. Of course, the conversation can be carried on in writing, with you and a part-ner passing a sheet of paper back and forth. This method gives you and the other person more time to think up suitable rhymes. Personally, I prefer to not use paper. I like the pressure of hav-ing to think up a rhyme on the spot. A round of "Rhyming Conversation" would sound like this:

   A: How are you?

   B: I don't have a clue. Where did you go?

   A: To the show. What about you?

B: I bought some glue. Did you go to the store?

A: No, I started to snore. What will you do tonight?

B: I have to catch my flight.

I kept my example simple, using only one-syllable rhyming words, which are called **masculine rhymes.** But you can certainly make the game a bit more interesting by using longer rhyming words like *mother/another,* which are called (can you guess?) **feminine rhymes.** However, remember that this is a game that is fun when there is back and forth, so don't confound* your partner by giving her impossible words for which to find rhymes.

MAKE IT FUNNY

One of my favorite games is "Tom Swifties." It gets its name from Tom Swift, a young action hero that kids in the 1930s and 1940s couldn't get enough of. He appeared in a series of books that described his hair-raising exploits and by-

*__Confound__ is a verb that used to mean "to destroy" but now means "to confuse."

the-skin-of-his-teeth escapes. The author of these books had a habit of always using an adverb after the verb *said* whenever he wrote dialogue, as in, *"We'd better get out of here," Tom said hurriedly.*

The word game, however, always includes a pun or play on words. For example, "I keep banging my head on things," Tom said *bashfully*, or "I have to renew my subscription," Tom said *periodically*. Get it? Do you notice the plays on words in these sentences?

Here are some "Tom Swifties" for you to try. Find the word from the list that best fits in the blank at the end of each sentence.

offhandedly   explosively   listlessly   gravely
frankly   absently   sourly   bluntly

1. "There's too much vinegar in my salad dressing," Tom said _____.
2. "I think I'll skip school tomorrow," Tom said _____.
3. "This pencil is dull," Tom said _____.
4. "That's the last time I'll pet a shark," Tom said _____.
5. "I don't like hot dogs," Tom said _____.

6. "Quick! I need some dynamite," Tom said _____.

7. "I'll try to dig it up for you," Tom said _____.

8. "I forgot what to buy," Tom said _____.

Now that you have the hang of "Tom Swifties," have some fun with your friends by coming up with your own. And don't forget to write the good ones in your notebook!

OPPOSITES

Once you have the hang of how to write a syn-
onym poem and writing about how things are the
same, try to do the opposite: Write about how
things are different. Sound confusing? It's not.
Just think "opposite." It's like looking at yourself
in the mirror. That ugly mosquito bite that's on
the right side of your nose will be on the left side
of your mirror nose. That bright green cast on
your broken right arm will suddenly be on your
left arm. Get it? Think "opposite."

Model Poems

1

What is the opposite of sunning on a beach?
Hiding in an igloo out of reach
Or diving deep in a frigid sea
Maybe sitting high in a coconut tree
Running and sliding on the snow
Or gliding away on a glacial ice floe.

2

What is the opposite of running away?
Staying home for another day.

3

The opposite of my little brother
Is getting the chance to pick another
Or having a sister in my house
Or having no siblings, just a pet mouse.

WHAT MAKES IT WORK

What's the first thing you notice about these opposites? True, they are quite clever (thank you very much), but what else do you notice? Do you notice the following qualities about these opposites?

- They are truly about things that are opposite. For example, "Hiding in an igloo out of reach" *is* the opposite of "sunning on the beach."

- They are written in couplets, which means that each poem will be two, four, or six lines long. They can be longer if you think you can do it!

- Many of the poems begin with a question, like *What is the opposite of unkind?* An opposite doesn't have to start with a question. But if it does, the rest of the poem answers that question.

- Like any good poem, each is built on specific details. Take a look at my third model poem. I didn't just write that my brother would "be something neat" or "something that I'd like."

Neither of those phrases is very specific. Instead, I wrote that the opposite of my brother would be "having no siblings, just a pet mouse."

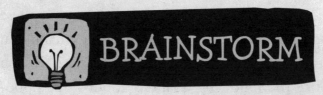

BRAINSTORM

A good way to brainstorm details to put into your poem is to create a web. In this case, you can write a question in the center of the web, like *What's the opposite of being left out?* As you think of words or phrases to answer this question — let your imagination run, but make sure you come up with specifics — write them in smaller circles at the ends of the branches coming off the main circle. Here's an example:

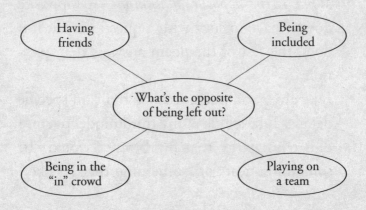

Now you try one:

WRITING TIPS

TIP #1

The first important thing you'll need to do when you try to write an opposite is to think of a good subject. That's important whenever you write a poem, but it's even more important when you're writing an opposite because not everything has an opposite. I'd suggest that you think of adjectives to start with because it might be easier to think of concrete things that are opposites, and not merely other adjectives. For example, if you chose the adjective *large* or *big* as your subject, your job would be to see what specific things you could list that are the opposite of *large.* On the list you might include things like: *mouse, ant, grain of sand, head of pin, speck of dust, a pebble caught in your shoe.* Once you have a list of specific things that might work in your poem, you can begin writing your draft.

TIP #2

Although the rhythm in opposite poems is not exact and precise, you'll need to juggle words as you go along to make sure that you have a smooth rhythm. This means, of course, that you'll need to read your poem out loud as you write it. When I was working on the draft for the first model poem, I wrote *Or diving in the sea,* but I could tell that that line had some problems. First of all, it was too short. Also, it didn't have a rhythm that was consistent with the rest of the poem. I changed that line to *Or diving deep into the sea,* but I still wasn't satisfied. I wanted to get something cold in the line, so I thought of the word *frigid* (which is a wonderful word, by the way) and decided to use it. As you can see, I wound up with *Or diving deep in a frigid sea,* which I liked very much.

If your opposites are going to be top-notch poems, you need to open your ears to the rhythm of poetry. See if you can fix the rhythm of the bold-faced lines in the two poems below. You can change words, take out words, and add words as you see fit.

What is the opposite of sitting around?
Climbing tall mountains in a single bound
Running in races and swimming the sea
And don't forget about learning how to ski

What is the opposite of having a friend?
Having no one on whom to depend
Getting no mail or calls on the phone
Eating your ice-cream cone all alone

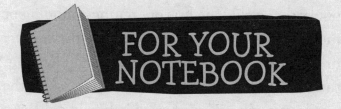

FOR YOUR NOTEBOOK

Good poets need to keep their eyes and ears open. Smart poets write down their observations in a notebook, which is exactly what you should be doing. You want to be a smart poet, don't you? Well then, start observing and taking notes for your opposite poems. For example, as you walk the hallways of your school, you might notice things that would be perfect for an opposite poem. You might notice how different boys and girls are in the way they dress and the way they act. You might notice how different you feel when you're in school as opposed to when the end-of-the-day bell sets you free. Things like these are great observations to include in your notebook and to write opposite poems about.

WORDPLAY

Although it's always wise to have a good dictionary and thesaurus handy, there are other books that yield long lists of exciting-sounding or musical words. Next time you visit the library, find a quiet corner, take a few field guides from the shelves, and be prepared to be amazed at the words you will find in them. Grab field guides to birds, insects, rocks, mushrooms, butterflies . . . the list goes on. For example, read out loud this list of bird names I discovered in a book on the birds of North America: *yelper, albatross, badgerbird,* and *dipper; gnatcatcher, goat sucker, grasssnipe,* and *gull; peewee, phoebe, pintail,* and *rook.*

You need not confine yourself to field guides. If you check the indices of many nonfiction books, you'll be rewarded with nifty words you've never heard of. Check out this list of fashion terms as you read it aloud: *apron, ascot, belt,* and *beret; cloak, coat, frock,* and *smock; jeans, jerkin, jersey,* and *jumper.*

Find the words, put them on a list, and listen to them sing and dance.

MAKE IT FUNNY

At the end of chapter four, I introduced you to "Tom Swifties," a game that helps you cultivate* your ability to write puns. "How's Business?" is another game designed to do the same thing.

In this game, one person asks a specific person, "How's business?" The other person must re-

---

*__Cultivate__ *has two meanings. The first meaning is "to prepare for raising crops," but it also means "to devote time and thought to."*

spond with a pun that is appropriate to the nature of the business. For example:

A: How's business, trash collector?

B: Picking up.

Get the pun? "Picking up," as in "picking up the trash." Okay, here's another:

A: How's business, florist?

B: Blooming.

You had to get the blooming pun. If you didn't, ask a friend to explain it to you. Then, try your hand at answering the following questions. Remember that your reply must be a pun appropriate to the business in the question. I've put the list of possible answers, in no particular order, following the questions. Try to come up with a pun before you look at the list for the answer.

1. How's business, carpet salesperson?
2. How's business, astronomer?
3. How's business, prizefighter?
4. How's business, knife maker?
5. How's business, pillow maker?
6. How's business, housewrecker?
7. How's business, weight watcher?
8. How's business, candle maker?

dull   down   sluggish   wicked
looking up   smashing   gaining   rugged

Can you think of other occupations and appropriate puns that go with them? Make a list and then try your own version of "How's Business?" with your friends.

SENRYU

Although you may not be familiar with senryu, you more than likely know its first cousin: haiku. That's because the haiku and the senryu grew up together in Japan a thousand years ago. Both types of poems were part of a longer poem called a renga. A renga began with a three-line stanza that was begun by a poet and posted in a tearoom. Other poets came along and added their short poems until the story was complete. Over time the parts of the renga — haiku and senryu — became individual poems, with one big difference. While haikus were always about nature and were generally serious, senryus were witty and clever and were written about human nature. I like to call them "haikus with attitude."

Model Poems

Diver's midair thought:
"Was there water in the pool?"
splash or splat below

Morning newspaper
leaves a lasting impression . . .
hands black with ink

Heading for a landing
skateboarder without helmet
knows his mom was right

Purse, makeup, backpack,
cell phone, cleats, water bottle . . .
no books in locker

WHAT MAKES
IT WORK

The basic senryu form is simple. Each senryu contains seventeen syllables that are divided into three lines of five, seven, and five syllables. It's generally descriptive and it's about human nature in the sense that it features the various things that humans do — like snoring, or dealing with a grumbling stomach, or drinking milk straight from the carton.

If you think of each poem as a postcard or a snapshot, that might help you narrow your subject. Just as the haiku captures a scene in nature, the senryu captures a scene from life. Don't try to tell a long story in your poem. Just take a picture with words.

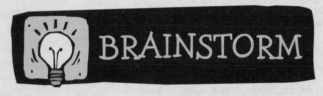

If you're like a lot of kids I know (and a lot of adults, come to think of it), you say to your friends, "I hate it when . . ." or "Did you ever notice how . . ." or "I wonder what would happen if . . ." Do these sound familiar? If so, you can use those observations to brainstorm senryus. But for now, just write down some ideas that build on these prompts. You can complete the prompts in your notebook, if that works for you. Look for things that are funny or **ironic**. (The word ironic describes a situation in which the meaning of a scene or event is contrary to what is apparent or expressed. The last model poem about a locker that has no room for books because there is so much other stuff in it is ironic.)

I wrote the first model poem after I'd been playing around with the notion of "what would happen if . . ." The second senryu I wrote after I noticed my smudged fingers from reading the newspaper and remembered that it was one of my pet peeves. The skateboarder senryu came about because I always wondered why kids bike or skateboard without helmets. The last poem was the result of observing my daughter's locker at school. It was jammed with so much stuff that she barely had room for her books!

WRITING TIPS

TIP #1

While it's true that the senryu follows a pattern, it is important to remember that you shouldn't be so taken up with following the pattern of the poem that you write a poem that doesn't sound right. In other words, if you need to add a syllable in a line or take out a syllable in another for the sake of the overall content of the poem, do it. Yes, you need to keep the senryu form in mind as you write and try to follow it, but the form shouldn't be a straightjacket that prevents you from saying what you'd like to say in your poem. In other words, you do have a little "wiggle room" when you write this particular form of poetry.

TIP #2

A lot of people think that when you write a poem, your draft has to look like a poem. That's not true. Your draft can look however you want it to. For example, you can write the first draft of a poem and have it look like a sentence or a paragraph. Then read it aloud and see where the line breaks should go. When you draft a senryu, you can write it as a sentence, then take a look at how you can break that sentence up into three lines. Then count the syllables and figure out where you need to cut or add. The most important thing is to get a good sense of what you want your poem to say as you draft it. You can worry about form later.

Take some of the observations you wrote in your notebook and see if you can capture the essence of one situation in seventeen syllables. Remember that this is practice, so don't worry if you have too many or too few syllables. The point is to look closely at the observation and see how you can eliminate words that aren't important. When you have written about five observations, try rewriting them as senryu.

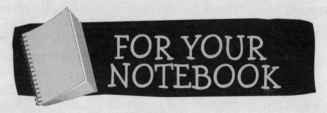

FOR YOUR NOTEBOOK

Even though senryus can be very clever and witty, you need to prepare to write one by doing some serious observing. Be on the lookout for things that strike you as funny about life. Also look for things that are annoying about life. Like dropping the soap when you are taking a shower and trying to pick up the slippery bar. Or squirting out way too much toothpaste and wishing you could get it back in the tube.

WORDPLAY

Although the alphabet has only twenty-six letters, combining those letters can produce all the words we'll ever need. Through the ages, people have fooled with the letters of the alphabet trying, for instance, to make the shortest possible sentence using all the letters. One poet wrote "The Siege of Belgrade," a twenty-six-line poem in which the first word of each line, and all subsequent words in the line, begin with a different letter of the alphabet. Here are the first two lines:

An Austrian army, awfully arrayed,
Boldly by battery besieged Belgrade.

While it is very difficult to write a poem like this one, you can make it simple. Here are the first few lines of another:

A is for apples, armadillos, and air
B is for butter, balloons, and bees
C is for cabbage, caboose, and camp
D is for donkey, dreidels, and dog

E is for elastics, earwax, and emu
F is for family, ferrets, and fracture

If you read these lines out loud, you can probably hear a rhythm you might want to use in your alphabet poem.

MAKE IT FUNNY

Another way to get a laugh with puns is to use them in a statement or in a **rhetorical question.** (Did you know that a rhetorical question is one that you don't expect to be answered?) For example:

Do you think they make dog biscuits out of "collie flour"?

Do you think a barber who works in a library is called a barbarian?

Do you suppose that sheep get their hair cut in a baa baa shop?

Do you think we can call a pumped-up pumpkin a jock o'lantern?

You can't beat our milk, but you can whip our cream.

I know a man who went to a mountain hotel for a rest and a change. The bellboy got the change, and the hotel got the rest.

To successfully use puns, you need to think of words that sound like something else. In the first question above, for example, *collie flour* sounds like *cauliflower.* In the third question, *baa baa shop* sounds like *barbershop.* So, when you think of puns, think of the sounds of the words. That's the key.

TEN LITTLE ALIENS

Of all the poems that I've written, "Ten Little Aliens" is probably the one that young writers like to hear me read the most. I remember how nervous I was when I read it to an audience of students for the first time. Much to my relief, they enjoyed it. In fact, when I make return visits to schools, it's the poem kids ask me to read again and again. Well, it didn't take me too long to figure out that if kids liked hearing the poem so much, they'd probably enjoy having the chance to write their own version of "Ten Little Aliens." So I always include it in any poetry writing workshop I do with young poets.

Model Poem

TEN LITTLE ALIENS

Ten little aliens landed feeling fine
One bought a hot tub and then there were nine

Nine little aliens stay up very late
One overslept and then there were eight

Eight little aliens took the name of Kevin
One died laughing and then there were seven

Seven little aliens studied magic tricks
One disappeared and then there were six

Six little aliens learned how to drive
One missed the exit and then there were five

Five little aliens polished the floor
One slipped and fell and then there were four

Four little aliens climbed a tall tree
One slipped and fell and then there were three

Three little aliens visited the zoo
One liked the ape and then there were two

Two little aliens baked in the sun
One got well-done and then there was one

One little alien went looking for fun
He never came back and then there were none

WHAT MAKES IT WORK

Like most rhyming poems, this one follows a pattern. But the pattern in this poem is more complicated than others. (More challenging and more fun, too, I might add.) I'm sure that you noticed right off the bat that this is another poem written in couplets. I hope you noticed that each couplet ends with a number. In other words, the first line must end with a word that rhymes with a number. But I hope you also noticed that:

- each couplet begins with a number;
- the number that begins each couplet decreases as the poem continues. (The first couplet begins with ten, the second couplet begins with nine, and so on.);
- the first word of the second line of each couplet is always the same: *One.*

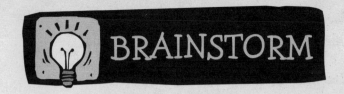

BRAINSTORM

As you know by now, to write your own successful version of "Ten Little Aliens," you need to be able to rhyme with numbers from nine to zero. Because each couplet will end with a specific number, you know that the last word of the first line of each couplet must rhyme with that same number.

To get started, brainstorm some words that rhyme with the numbers nine to zero. (Rhyme Warning: There are only half a dozen words that rhyme with *seven* and three of them are boys' names! Do you know what they are?)

WRITING TIPS

TIP #1

Although my poem is about aliens, yours certainly doesn't need to be. The important thing to remember is to tell a funny story. You could write about Ten Bratty Brothers, Ten Snotty Sisters, Ten Mellow Teachers, Ten Little Hamsters, Ten Music Lovers, or Ten Mountain Climbers. The topic is up to you. Find something that has the potential to be funny. That's why I picked aliens for my poem. I thought it would be funny if these creatures from outer space did "human" things.

The subject you choose need not have "little" in it. In fact, if you take another look at the topics I suggested above, only one of them has "little" in it. But you should also notice that each title does contain a two-syllable adjective that modifies the noun in the subject. That two-syllable word gives the first line of each couplet a smooth rhythm that is repeated throughout the poem. Also, if you pick a suitable adjective, it can help you write something funny. For example, if you decide to write about "Ten Mellow Teachers," your poem would be very funny if you can have one teacher in each line get stressed and then unhinged.

TIP #2

How can you make your poem funny? Well, I had aliens do human things. But there are other ways to make your poem funny. One good way is to carefully choose what your characters are going to do. For example, in one of my couplets, I have the aliens learn how to drive. What could I put in the second line that might be funny? I tried *One drove away,* but I wasn't thrilled with that. Then I tried *One bought a van,* which wasn't too bad. Then I came up with *One got lost,* which I liked very much. But I still thought I could do better, maybe by making that phrase more specific. And that's how I wound up with *One missed the exit.* Here are a few phrases that writing workshop students have suggested: *One lost his map, One lost his keys, One took a wrong turn, One needed a tune-up.* Can you think of other lines that would have been as funny or funnier?

PRACTICE

It might help you write your alien poem if you think of each couplet as a very tiny, teeny short story, just as I suggested with the jump-rope rhyme at the start of this book. In the first line of your story, there is a group of aliens doing something (for example, *Six little aliens learned how to drive.*). In the second line, one of them does something or something happens to one of them (for example, *One missed the exit*), and then there is one less *(and then there were five).* In a sense, the entire poem is like a novel with ten chapters. As you think of ideas for your poem, keep this structure in mind. Your poem will tell a story of what happens to ten _____.

If you fill in the blanks in the couplets below, you will be on the way to writing your own version of "Ten Little Aliens." You can write your answers in your notebook.

Ten little aliens stood in a _____
One got bored and then there were nine

Nine little aliens tried to walk _____
One was too dizzy then there were eight

Eight little aliens wanted to go to _____
One bought some wings and then there were
   seven

Seven little aliens purchased some _____
One was allergic and then there were six

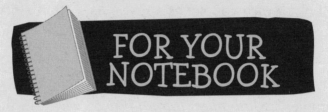

FOR YOUR NOTEBOOK

Write this phrase at the top of a page in your notebook: TEN LITTLE . . . WHAT? Use that page to list some topics that you might want to explore in your poem. Look around for a subject. Do you see animals that would work in your poem? Certain kinds of people at school? How about somebody in your family? Don't forget to put your imagination to work on this one. That's what I did when I chose "aliens" for my poem.

WORDPLAY

I remember reading a comic strip in the Sunday newspaper when I was a kid that cracked me up. In the strip two characters were talking. Their conversation went something like this:

A: I have an uncle who lives in Walla Walla.

B: What does he do for a living?

A: He sells bonbons door to door.

B: How's business?

A: So so.

This got me thinking about all the words we have in our language that repeat their sound, like the words in the comic strip. In some, the initial sound of the second part changes, as with the following words:

bowwow	willy-nilly	walkie-talkie
blackjack	boohoo	teeny-weeny

By the way, these kinds of words use **assonance,** the same vowel sound but a different initial consonant.

Then there are the words in which you keep the same initial consonant but change the vowel sound — **alliteration.** Here are some examples:

ticktock	wishy-washy	creepy-crawly
seesaw	zigzag	mishmash
knickknack	riffraff	fiddle-faddle

Can you think of other words or phrases in which sounds are repeated like the examples in these lists? Most of the words on my lists have something of a nifty comical sound to them, so using words like them in your poems could put a smile on the face of your reader. Try to keep a list in your notebook of words that have repeated sounds. Then see if you can find a place for them in one of your poems.

MAKE IT FUNNY

Speaking of neat-sounding words, here's a good one: **oxymoron.** Do you know what it means? No, it has nothing to do with a stupid ox. It's a phrase that contains two contradictory words. Some of them are funny. Here are some samples of oxymorons:

fish farm	double solitaire
ill health	clearly confused
real potential	plastic silverware
12-ounce pound cake	original copies
sanitary landfill	small crowd
unbiased opinion	open secret

I know a lot of students (and teachers) who think *cafeteria food* is an oxymoron. Some people consider *polite salesman, friendly takeover, holy war,* and *taped live* to be oxymorons. Have you noticed any oxymorons? Have you used them? Have your friends? Like *a definite maybe?* Like *pretty ugly?* Pay attention to what's said at school and around your home. When you hear a good oxymoron, write it down in your notebook. Who knows? You might be able to include them in poems. You might even be able to write a whole poem that consists of oxymorons.

I LIKE THAT STUFF

It's no secret to any of you rhymesters that it seems easier to find rhymes for one-syllable words — like *ache, bake, wake, quake* — than it is to find rhymes for longer words — like *brother, smother, another*. This is one of the things I enjoy about "I Like That Stuff" — it asks you to find feminine rhymes, rhyming words of more than one syllable. I got the idea for this poem from "Stufferation," a humorous poem written by British poet Adrian Mitchell. I liked it so much that I began using it with my writing students with some hilarious results.

Model Poem

I LIKE THAT STUFF

by Writing Workshop students

Children play on it
Adults lay on it
Sand
I like that stuff

Cats curl in it
Plants unfurl in it
Sun
I like that stuff

Cakes are smothered with it
Twix are covered with it
Chocolate
I like that stuff

Frowns are fixed by it
Friends are mixed by it
Smiles
I like that stuff

Parents grow it
Kids mow it
Grass
I like that stuff

Vegetarians eat them
Grillers heat them
Vegetables
I like that stuff

WHAT MAKES IT WORK

This poem seems more complicated than it really is. First of all, each stanza is four lines long. But look at a stanza. You'll see that the fourth line, "I like that stuff," is the title of the poem and the **refrain** that is repeated at the end of every stanza. The third line is the subject of the stanza. The first two lines are the only lines that you have to actually "write." The opening couplet presents a challenge because of the feminine rhyme, but there's no doubt that you can do it. Just remember that it's not simply the *it* that rhymes. Take a look at these two rhymes from the model poem:

play on it/lay on it and *curl in it/unfurl in it.* Notice how each has three syllables that rhyme. That's the type of feminine rhyme that you need to use in your opening couplet.

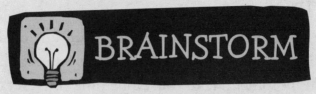

Although it's a good idea to write about something that you react to, you can also write about a topic that doesn't mean a lot to you, as long as you can find something to write about. For example, the girl who wrote the stanza about sand wasn't a sand lover. But she liked to play around with words, so she brainstormed ideas by thinking of rhymes. When she came up with *play* and *lay,* she went from there. Her first thought was *blanket,* but she wasn't happy with that, so she kept playing around until she thought of *sand.* As you brainstorm, don't let my suggestions lock you into one way of looking at the poem. Let your imagination go and jot down whatever comes to mind. You may be pleasantly surprised. I know I've been surprised by brainstorming more times than I can count.

WRITING TIPS

TIP #1

I suggest you start with the third line of the stanza. That's the subject. Pick a subject that means something to you. Something you react to. Something you like. Something that's a pet peeve. Many of my writing students ask if the poem has to be "true," how they really feel about the subject. The answer is, of course, no. "I Like That Stuff" is supposed to be a humorous poem and not the story of your life.

TIP #2

Once you've decided on a topic, think about that subject. What does it do? What do people do with it? To it? What qualities does it have? For example, the model poem about chocolate begins with two things that chocolate does: it smothers cakes and covers candy bars. Reread the model poems and see how these subjects were handled. Then get your notebook and start jotting down the qualities of your subject. You may be surprised to discover a rhyme somewhere along the

way. If the rhyme doesn't appear, take some time
to look for one.

Play around with feminine rhyme. Turn to a
blank page in your notebook and start thinking
of multisyllable words and phrases that rhyme.
Anything goes: *float in it/boat in it; groove to it/
move to it; improve them/remove them; shout it/
scout it; caught it/bought it.* You might thumb
through a rhyming dictionary to get some ideas.
As I mentioned above, this is another way to
come to the subject of your poem. For example,
take a look at this rhyme: *float in it/boat in it.*
That combination leads me to think about water
as the subject of a stanza. Maybe something like
this:

Captains boat it in
Chubby swimmers float in it
Water
I like that stuff

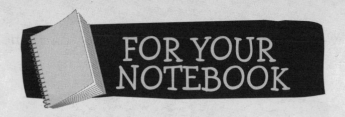

FOR YOUR NOTEBOOK

Your notebook is the perfect place to keep track of topics that might work in "I Like That Stuff." I have had writing workshop students use the form of this poem, but change the point of view and instead write "I Hate That Stuff." You could divide a page in your notebook down the middle and write I HATE THAT STUFF at the top of one column and I LIKE THAT STUFF at the top of the other. Then save topics in the appropriate columns.

WORDPLAY

It's always nice to add new words to your vocabulary. They help you understand what you read, and the right words certainly make writing more interesting. Here's a word game to increase your store of words. The directions are simple. To start, write the alphabet down the center of a page in your notebook. To the left of each letter, write an agreeable word that starts with that letter. To the right of each letter, write a disagreeable word that starts with that letter. Here are some examples to get you started:

agreeable	A	antisocial
brave	B	bumbling
clever	C	careless
diligent	D	disruptive
easygoing	E	egotistical
friendly	F	frosty
generous	G	grumpy
hilarious	H	huffy
ingenious	I	impatient
jolly	J	jejune*

I'd suggest that you write the alphabet down the page first, and then see how many words you can immediately write down. Do some thinking and resist the urge to take the easy way out by writing down the first thing that comes to mind. Instead, write down interesting words. This is a perfect time to drag out the dictionary that Aunt Mildred sent you for your last birthday. Cruising the dictionary is a good way to learn new words.

* **Jejune** is a French word that means "childish, lacking maturity."

 MAKE IT FUNNY

At the end of the section on senryus, I suggested that you write a parody of a nursery rhyme. You could also write a parody of a popular song. Remember, for the parody to be funny, the reader (or listener, if you have the guts to sing your parody) must know the original song that you're spoofing. For example, here's a parody of "Jingle Bells":

Jingle Bells

Batman smells

Robin laid an egg.

Batmobile lost a wheel

And Penguin did ballet.

Hey!

Make a list of popular songs that you can parody. Think of some holiday songs — like "Rudolph, the Red-Nosed Reindeer" and "Here Comes Santa Claus" — or some rounds — like "Row, Row, Row Your Boat" — or other songs that most people will recognize — like "Twinkle, Twinkle, Little Star" and "Mary Had a Little Lamb."

IF I COULD PUT
A CURSE ON YOU

I remember very clearly the day that the idea for this poem came to me. I'd been having a bad day. Nothing horrible had happened, just a lot of those small annoying things that drive me crazy. The traffic was stalled because of a fender bender. The lady in front of me in the fewer-than-12-items express line at the supermarket had more than a dozen things in her shopping cart. My grocery bag split when I got caught in a downpour. Dumb little things, I know, but they made me nuts. I was mad at the world. So I decided to write a poem that would put a curse on people. Maybe that would make me feel better! Oh, I'm not a mean person who wants horrible things to happen to people. We have plenty of people like that in the world already. I just wanted to write a poem filled with annoying things that I wanted to befall others. And after writing this poem, I felt much better! This is one of the positive side effects of writing: It can lift some of the burdens that we carry on our shoulders.

Model Poem

IF I COULD PUT A CURSE ON YOU

If I could put a curse on you
I would have a laugh or two

May your gym shorts fall below your knees
May your locker fill with killer bees

May you bust a spoke on your new bike
May your girlfriend tell you, "Take a hike!"

May you muff the science on the test
May you skulk around the halls half-dressed

May your parents find out what you did
May the bully find out where you hid

May your lunch get purloined and eaten
May your favorite teams get beaten

May you get a pimple on your nose
May you grow an extra pair of toes

Oh, if I could put a curse on you
I would have a laugh or two

But only someone who's a brat
Would do a rotten thing like that

WHAT MAKES IT WORK

You'll notice that this poem follows a pattern like many of the other rhyming poems in this book. Hopefully you've noticed that the poem is written in couplets. Do you see how many of the lines begin with the same word or two? The rhythm is pretty consistent throughout the poem. Each line in the main part of the poem contains a curse that I want to befall the reader. But another important thing to notice is that my "curses" are really silly annoying things — not terrible things — that I want to happen to the reader. Keep that in mind when you write your poem.

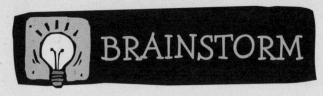

BRAINSTORM

Since the bulk of the poem is the curses, begin by brainstorming what curses you would like to include in your poem. One way to start your list is to think of the things that annoy you, like *May your dog roll over in the mud* or *May your sister snoop in your room*. Even more fun is to let your imagination think of some great exaggerations, like *May your nose drop off and roll away* or *May your ears fill up with candle wax*. I love to come up with diabolical curses!

WRITING TIPS

TIP #1

Be on the lookout for places in this poem (and every poem, for that matter) where you can include vivid language. For example, in the following practice section I use the line *May you smash your mother's favorite plate*. In the draft of that line, I'd written *May you drop your mother's fa-*

vorite dish. I changed the verb to make it more vivid and expressive. *Smash* creates a more vivid image in the reader's mind than *drop*. And I thought that *plate* sounded "more valuable" than *dish*. In another example, I wrote *May your nose drop off and roll away,* although my first draft was *May your nose fall off and roll away.* Again, I think *drop* is much more expressive than *fall*.

TIP #2

Each line in your poem should create an image in the reader's mind. Using vivid verbs is one way to do that. But more than that, you should choose curses that include sense words to create an image for the reader. For example, *May you smash your mother's favorite plate* is something that we can see and hear. The same is true for *May your nose drop off and roll away.* Plus this line has a pretty high Yuck Factor going for it. By that I mean that when someone hears that line, they're apt to let out an "Oh, yuck!" because it creates a clear (and yucky) picture.

PRACTICE

Since rhythm and rhyme are such important parts of most rhyming poems (duh!), it's always good to practice those two aspects of a poem. Below are a few lines that could go in a curse poem. Try to write a rhyming line to go with each one. Write your lines in your notebook:

1. May your nose drop off and roll away
   May _____

2. May you smash your mother's favorite plate
   May _____

3. May your brother listen to your calls
   May _____

4. May you lose your father's favorite tool
   May _____

5. May your pillow smell like rotten cheese
   May _____

When you're comfortable with the rhythm and rhyme of this poem, start a draft of your own version. Of course, you can use any of the ideas you dreamed up in the Brainstorm and Practice sections. Just don't forget to have fun with the poem and not use it as a way to truly wish other people harm.

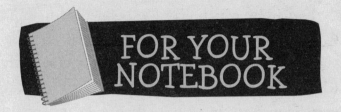
FOR YOUR NOTEBOOK

This is another poem that can easily come from your observations, so be attentive to what's going on around you and keep your notebook (or at least a scrap of paper) handy so you can jot down ideas for a curse poem. To remind yourself to be on the lookout for curses, you might want to write CURSES at the top of a page in your notebook and jot down anything appropriate that comes to mind. You can also think of things that would be curses if they happened to you, then write them as something that you'd like to happen to someone else. You could wind up with quite a list of hilarious curses.

Earlier in this book, I explained "Rhyming Conversation," a rhyming game involving a back-and-forth among a group of players. "Guess My Rhyme" is another such game, although in it the participants ask questions, then give answers in rhyme. Here's how it works: One player starts the game by saying something like, "I have a word that rhymes with ___" and says a word, like *bat*. The other players then take turns trying to guess his word by asking questions about the mystery word but without ever actually saying the word. A player might ask, "Is it something that covers my head?" The first player would figure out what word his opponent has in mind and use it in his rhyming reply: "No, it's not a hat." The game continues in that fashion. Here's a continuation of that game:

> C: Is it something to wipe my feet on?
>
> A: No, it's not a mat.
>
> D: Is it a rodent with a long tail?
>
> A: No, it's not a rat.
>
> E: Is it a feline?

A: No, it's not a cat.

F: Is it a piece of equipment used in baseball?

A: No, it's not a bat.

G: Is it an animal that flies at night?

A: Yes! It's a bat.

Although this game works best with one-syllable words, you can try it with longer words.

MAKE IT FUNNY

By now, you've noticed that you can get a laugh if you use homonyms in a clever way. Another way to use homonyms is in funny definitions, sometimes called "daffy-nitions." Here are a few examples:

Intense: where campers sleep

Eclipse: what the gardener does to your hedge

Heroes: what a guy in a boat does

Control: a short, ugly prison inmate

Polynesia: memory loss in parrots

Toad: what happens to an illegally parked frog

Each of these "daffy-nitions" gets its humor from the use of homonyms. *Intense* sounds like *in tents. Eclipse* sounds like *'e clips. Heroes* sounds like *He rows.* And so on.

As I suggested earlier in this book, you can get started using homonyms by listening carefully to words and phrases and being alert to what they sound like. When you think you've found a pair of good homonyms, say them out loud. Can you hear the similarity? Will someone else hear the humor in it? Save your ideas in your notebook.

NONSENSE ALPHABET

Although most people associate Edward Lear with the limerick, he wrote some of the classic humorous poems of the English language, including "The Owl and the Pussy-Cat." He also wrote a number of, what he called, "Nonsense Alphabets." Here's an example from one such alphabet:

A was an Ape,
Who stole some white Tape,
And tied up his Toes
In four beautiful Bows.

C was a Camel,
You rode on his Hump,
And if you fell off,
You came down such a Bump!

Of course, when I read some of Lear's "Nonsense Alphabets," I just had to take a crack at writing one of my own.

Model Poem

NONSENSE ALPHABET

A was an Apple,
wherein lived a worm.
Bite to the center
If you need to confirm.

B was a book
Sulking on a shelf,
Abridged, truncated
And no longer itself.

C was a Cantaloupe
Growing on a vine
A farmer dropped it
Trying to carry nine.

D was a doorbell
Ready to be poked
It cried out so shrill
But always felt provoked.

E was an evergreen
Growing in the heights
Till it was cut down,
Strung with tinsel and lights.

F was a flamingo
Orange and gawky
Tired of standing
It gets downright squawky.

G was a gnat
Pesky little bug
I grabbed in my fist
Gnot exactly a hug.

H was a hydrant
Of course, painted red
When dogs sauntered by
It was filled with dread.

I was an igloo
Solid and frozen
When I pick a house
It won't be the one chosen.

WHAT MAKES IT WORK

If you listen carefully to this poem, you will hear that it contains many of the elements of the humorous poetry that you've tried in this guide.

This alphabet poem has the overall structure of the alphabet. Each stanza features one thing that begins with each letter of the alphabet and is four lines long. What else do you notice about the way this poem is written? The first line begins with the letter that is the "subject" of the stanza. Although the first line has four or five syllables, the syllable count in the other lines looks like this: lines two and three each have five syllables, and line four has six syllables. And lines two and four rhyme, giving the poem a rhyme scheme *abcb*. Each stanza gives some specifics about the subject of the stanza, e.g., the igloo is "solid and frozen," the gnat is a "pesky little bug." Of course, you want to work in something funny or clever in each stanza, like the doorbell crying out when provoked, or the hydrant getting nervous when dogs approach.

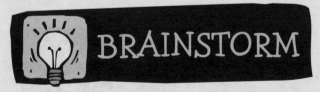

If you're going to write a nonsense alphabet, you need to find twenty-six things to write about, all starting with a different letter. You might want to begin by brainstorming a list of twenty-six things. In your notebook, you can write each letter of the alphabet on a line to the left of the red margin and, on that same line, some items that begin with that letter.

It will be easy to find items for most letters, but you'd better watch out when you get toward the end of the alphabet, especially *q*, *y*, and *z*. Give yourself some poetic license. In other words, since you are writing a humorous poem, it's okay for you to play around with the letters and their sounds. For example, we know the word *excuse* doesn't start with an *x*. However, we also know that it *sounds* like it does. So, you might want to use *xcuse* or *xercise* for your *x* words. Have some fun with your poetic license. It can add surprise to your poems. Look through the dictionary for help. It holds tons of words that would fit into your "Nonsense Alphabet."

WRITING TIPS

TIP #1

Once you've decided which item you are going to write about — for example, *A was an apple* — you should ask yourself what's going to happen to this apple. Can you think of something funny that the apple can do? Can you think of something silly that can happen to the apple? It may help you to write out your idea. It doesn't have to rhyme or have the appropriate rhythm. Just write out your idea. What does it look like? Read your idea aloud. What does it sound like? You'll probably find yourself playing around with your idea: crossing out this word, changing that word. Slowly, a stanza will begin to take shape. Keep working at it until you get it just right.

TIP #2

Try to write stanzas for six letters of the alphabet before you go back and read through what you've done. Make each stanza as good as you can make it, but don't read over all of them until you've written a handful. Then read them aloud in order. Can you hear the rhythm? Can you hear the rhymes in lines two and four? Do you feel yourself smiling as you read them? These are all tests you should put your stanzas through. If something's amiss, find out what it is and fix it.

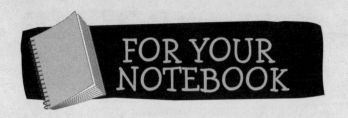

When you were a kid, you probably read some books with titles like, *Barnyard Animals A to Z* or *Alphabet City,* books in which each letter of the alphabet was represented by an object or a person on the farm or in the city. You might want to try the same thing with your "Nonsense Alphabet." Can you think of places or areas that would be rich with items that you could include in your poem? Can you, for instance, write your "Nonsense Alphabet" about school? Or sports? Or music, animals, or weather?

Use a page in your notebook and write NONSENSE ALPHABET across the top. When you think you've found a good subject, jot it down on the list. Don't expect a perfect list, where all the subjects will make great poems. The point of the list is to gather ideas that you can later consider when you're looking for a topic for a poem. Use your imagination!

WORDPLAY

One of the classic nonsense poems is "Jabber-wocky" by Lewis Carroll, the man who wrote *Alice in Wonderland*. (In fact, he wrote some other fine nonsense poems that you can find in your library.) The poem is remarkable because he fills it with words that aren't recognizable. Below are the first few stanzas. Read them aloud and see what you notice about the poem.

'Twas brillig, and the slithy toves
Did gyre and gimble in the wabe;
All mimsy were the borogoves,
And the mome raths outgrabe.

"Beware the Jabberwock, my son!
The jaws that bite, the claws that catch!
Beware the Jubjub bird, and shun
The frumious Bandersnatch!"

He took his vorpal sword in hand:
Long time the manxome foe he sought —
So rested he by the Tumtum tree,
And stood awhile in thought.

You probably noticed the poem *sounds* like it makes sense even though many of the words are nonsense words. The poem has regular rhythm, and lines two and four rhyme in each stanza.

Why not try to write your own opening stanza of a poem that follows the pattern that Carroll used in "Jabberwocky"? Have some fun making up words that sound like real words.

MAKE IT FUNNY

Like the "Tom Swifties" that I asked you to fool with at the end of the section on writing "I'd Like to," this exercise is based on puns. It's called "Don't Worry," and here are some examples:

Don't worry, baldy . . . you're smooth.

Don't worry, bank . . . you're safe.

Don't worry, doctor . . . you've got the patience.

Don't worry, hunter . . . you're game.

Don't worry, printer . . . I'm not your type.

Don't worry, clock . . . I've got the time.

Don't worry, bread . . . I'm well-bred.

Don't worry, ocean . . . I'll wave.

Don't worry, tree . . . I'll leave.
Don't worry, carpet . . . you'll floor 'em.

Be on the lookout for puns and write them down in your notebook. Then read over your list and see how you can use the puns.

SOME LAST WORDS

I hope that you've had some fun as you worked your way through this book. I hope, too, that you've learned a thing or two about writing poetry along the way. Although many of the poems that you learned about in this book follow a specific pattern or form, you should feel free to experiment with variations of the forms that I included in this book. Who knows? You might even invent a new form of poetry!

On the last few pages of this book, I've included writing lines. As you read through this guide, jot down any ideas that you want to save for a poem.

In case you're looking for a list of books to read to get new ideas about the possibilities of poetry, this is your lucky day. I've included a reading list at the end of this book. Although my list is a great place to start, branch out and explore the poetry section of your library. Chances are good that great treasures await you.

As you continue to work on your writing — remember, that's the only way to get better — don't forget that you are writing poetry and not gags or party jokes. In other words, don't settle for the first words that fall out of your wild imagination. Make an effort to find the best words for each poem you write.

Finally, share your poems. Write a poem on a card and give it to someone who might enjoy it. Send a poem by e-mail. Write a good one on a note and pass it to a buddy during study hall. Any good poem you write is worth sharing, but a funny poem might be just what a person needs to lift her spirits. We all need to smile more, and a funny poem might be just what we need.

Keep writing. And have fun while you're at it!

SUGGESTED
READING LIST

Cole, Joanna. *Miss Mary Mack.* A collection of jump-rope rhymes.

Lear, Edward. *The Complete Verse and Other Nonsense.* The man wrote more than the limericks for which he is widely known.

Lewis, J. Patrick. *Riddle-icious.* A fabulous collection of riddles; *Doodle Dandies.* A collection of concrete poems. Make sure to look for other books by Lewis.

McNaughton, Colin. *Making Friends with Frankenstein: A Book of Monstrous Poems and Pictures; Wish You Were Here and I Wasn't: A Book of Poems and Pictures for Globe Trotters.* He's written lots of books full of laughs.

Nesbitt, Kenn. *The Aliens Have Landed; Sailing Off to Singapore.* The new kid of the humorous poetry block. Check him out.

Prelutsky, Jack. *It's Raining Pigs & Noodles; A Pizza the Size of the Sun; The Dragons are Singing Tonight.* The man of a thousand laughs.

Sierra, Judy. *There's a Zoo in Room 22.* Lots of laughs, especially if you like animals.

Wilbur, Richard. *Opposites; More Opposites.*